I0426057

May 2012

RURAL HOUSING SERVICE

Efforts to Identify and Reduce Improper Rental Assistance Payments Could Be Enhanced

GAO

Accountability ★ Integrity ★ Reliability

May 2012

RURAL HOUSING SERVICE

Efforts to Identify and Reduce Improper Rental Assistance Payments Could be Enhanced

GAO

Accountability * Integrity * Reliability

Highlights

Highlights of GAO-12-624, a report to congressional requesters

Why GAO Did This Study

RHS, an agency within USDA, paid property owners about $1 billion in fiscal year 2011 to help more than 270,000 low-income rural tenants afford rental housing. Each year, some of RHS's rental subsidy payments are improper—that is, too high or too low. Federal requirements regarding improper payments are set forth in statute and in OMB guidance. GAO was asked to review (1) the extent to which RHS has examined the sources and magnitude of improper rental assistance payments, (2) RHS's compliance with requirements and guidance concerning improper payments, and (3) potential lessons RHS could learn from HUD efforts to identify and reduce improper rental assistance payments. To do this work, GAO analyzed agency data and documents; reviewed statutes and guidance; and interviewed RHS, HUD, and OMB officials.

What GAO Recommends

To help reduce improper payments caused by unreported tenant income, GAO suggests that Congress should consider authorizing RHS access to HHS's New Hires database and recommends that RHS develop proposed legislation to gain access to SSA benefits data. GAO also recommends that USDA submit RHS's method for estimating improper payments to OMB for review and that RHS take steps to consistently apply procedures for classifying payments as improper, examine improper payments made on behalf of deceased tenants or caused by payment processing errors, and hold agency managers accountable for reducing improper payments. USDA said it generally agreed with GAO's recommendations.

View GAO-12-624. For more information, contact Mathew Scirè at (202) 512-8678 or scirem@gao.gov.

What GAO Found

The Rural Housing Service (RHS) has identified improper rental assistance payments caused by certain sources of errors, but its reported error rate (total amount improperly paid divided by program outlays) may understate the magnitude of the problem. RHS has identified improper payments resulting from inaccurate calculations of tenant subsidies and incomplete supporting documents. From fiscal years 2007 through 2010, RHS reduced its reported error rate from 3.95 percent (representing $35 million in errors) to 1.48 percent (representing $15 million in errors). However, these figures may be understated because RHS has not estimated improper payments due to unreported tenant income, and it lacks the authority to match tenant data to federal income data for this purpose. These data include the Department of Health and Human Services' (HHS) New Hires database and the Social Security Administration's (SSA) data on benefits payments. RHS has proposed legislation to gain access to the HHS data but not the SSA data. Additionally, RHS has not recently estimated payment processing errors and has not strictly adhered to procedures for classifying payments as improper. Further, in 2008, RHS began excluding improper payments of less than $100 from its estimated error rates. However, it did not submit this change to the Office of Management and Budget (OMB), which is responsible for approving agency methodologies for estimation. As a result, RHS lacks assurance that its approach is appropriate.

RHS uses required statistical methods for estimating improper payments but has not fully met requirements for reporting on, reducing, and recovering such payments. Consistent with the Improper Payments Information Act of 2002, as amended, and OMB guidance, RHS examines a statistically valid sample of payments and generates estimates with an acceptable level of precision. RHS also has reported required information, such as actions to address payment errors. However, RHS did not fully comply with the requirement to implement and report steps for holding agency managers accountable for reducing improper payments. In addition, although OMB cites data matching as a way to reduce payment errors, RHS has not used data already available from SSA to detect payments made on behalf of deceased tenants. Further, RHS has yet to institute a recovery audit program in accordance with the Improper Payments Elimination and Recovery Act of 2010, although it plans to do so sometime in 2012. These shortcomings negatively affect the integrity of RHS's subsidy payments.

The Department of Housing and Urban Development's (HUD) use of data matching to reduce improper payments in its rental assistance programs illustrates the potential benefits and challenges of this technique for RHS. HUD developed a web-based system that allows authorized HUD staff and program administrators (e.g., public housing agencies) to match tenant information to HHS's New Hires database and SSA benefits data. According to HUD, the system has helped to reduce income reporting errors and has contributed to a more than threefold decline in total improper payments from fiscal years 2000 through 2010. Negotiating a data-sharing agreement with one agency and fully implementing the data matching system took several years. Additionally, HUD provides extensive guidance, training, and technical assistance to program administrators to help ensure effective use of the system.

_____ United States Government Accountability Office

Contents

Letter		1
	Background	4
	RHS Has Identified and Reduced Certain Types of Payment Errors, but Its Reported Error Rate May Understate the Magnitude of the Problem	8
	RHS Uses Required Statistical Methods for Estimating Improper Payments but Has Not Fully Met Reporting, Reduction, and Recovery Requirements	17
	HUD's Efforts Illustrate Potential Benefits and Challenges of Data Matching	26
	Conclusions	33
	Matter for Congressional Consideration	36
	Recommendations for Executive Action	36
	Agency Comments and Our Evaluation	37
Appendix I	Objectives, Scope, and Methodology	39
Appendix II	Comments from the Department of Agriculture	44
Appendix III	GAO Contact and Staff Acknowledgments	46
Tables		
	Table 1: RHS Estimates of Gross Improper Rental Assistance Payments and Error Rates, Fiscal Years 2007-2010	10
	Table 2: RHS Reporting on Improper Payments in Response to OMB Requirements	19
	Table 3: Status of RHS Corrective Actions Regarding Improper Rental Assistance Payments	22
Figures		
	Figure 1: Basic Steps in the RHS Rental Subsidy Process, as of April 2012	6
	Figure 2: Potential Sources of Payment Errors Examined and Not Examined by RHS's Improper Payments Audit, as of April 2012	11

Figure 3: Distribution of Improper Payments in RHS's Sample of
Fiscal Year 2010 Payments   15
Figure 4: Estimated RHS Improper Rental Assistance Payments in
Fiscal Year 2010 Including and Excluding Errors Less
Than $100   16

Abbreviations

CSC	Centralized Servicing Center
EIV	Enterprise Income Verification System
HHS	Department of Health and Human Services
HUD	Department of Housing and Urban Development
IPERA	Improper Payments Elimination and Recovery Act of 2010
IPIA	Improper Payments Information Act of 2002
MFIS	Multi-Family Information System
NAHMA	National Affordable Housing Management Association
OIG	Office of the Inspector General
OMB	Office of Management and Budget
PAR	Performance and Accountability Report
PHA	public housing agency
RFP	request for proposals
RHIIP	Rental Housing Integrity Improvement Project
RHS	Rural Housing Service
SSA	Social Security Administration
USDA	U.S. Department of Agriculture

United States Government Accountability Office
Washington, DC 20548

May 31, 2012

The Honorable Charles Grassley
Ranking Member
Committee on the Judiciary
United States Senate

The Honorable Judy Biggert
Chair
Subcommittee on Insurance, Housing
    and Community Opportunity
Committee on Financial Services
House of Representatives

The Honorable Shelley Moore Capito
Chairwoman
Subcommittee on Financial Institutions
    and Consumer Credit
Committee on Financial Services
House of Representatives

In fiscal year 2011, the Rural Housing Service (RHS) of the U.S.
Department of Agriculture (USDA) paid about $1.1 billion in subsidies
under the Section 521 rental assistance program to help more than a
quarter of a million very low- and low-income rural tenants afford decent
rental housing.[1] The properties in which the tenants live were created
through other RHS programs that provide low-interest loans for the
development of multifamily housing. RHS pays rental subsidies to the
owners of the properties to limit tenants' rent payments to 30 percent of
the household's adjusted monthly income. However, each year, some of
RHS's subsidy payments are improper because they should not have
been made or were made in an incorrect amount.

Like other executive branch agencies, RHS is required to comply with
requirements designed to enhance the accuracy and integrity of federal
payments. Under the Improper Payments Information Act of 2002 (IPIA),

---

[1]Very low income is defined as below 50 percent of the area median income; low income
is from 50 to 80 percent of area median income.

GAO-12-624 RHS Improper Payments

agencies are required to estimate annual amounts improperly paid and to report these estimates and actions taken to reduce them.[2] The Improper Payments Elimination and Recovery Act of 2010 (IPERA) amended IPIA and, among other things, expanded requirements for recovering overpayments.[3] The Director of the Office of Management and Budget (OMB) prescribes guidance for agencies to use in implementing IPIA, as amended.

In prior work, we reported that the Department of Housing and Urban Development (HUD), which paid over $32 billion in rental subsidies in fiscal year 2010, had substantially reduced the amount of improper payments in its three rental assistance programs.[4] Specifically, we reported that HUD paid an estimated $3.4 billion in improper rent subsidies in fiscal year 2000 but cut that amount to about $1.5 billion in fiscal year 2005. Since that time, HUD has made continuing efforts to reduce improper payments for these programs, including the use of data matching techniques to help ensure payment accuracy.

You asked us to examine RHS's efforts to address improper rental assistance payments in the Section 521 program. Accordingly, this report addresses (1) the extent to which RHS has examined the sources and magnitude of improper rental assistance payments; (2) the extent to which RHS has complied with applicable requirements and guidance for estimating, reporting, reducing, and recovering improper payments; and (3) potential lessons RHS could learn from HUD efforts that have helped to identify and reduce improper rental assistance payments.

To determine the extent to which RHS has examined the sources and magnitude of improper payments, we reviewed RHS's improper payments audits of the rental assistance program for fiscal years 2004 through 2010 (the most recent audit available at the time of our review). We reviewed RHS's audit procedures and examined the policies governing RHS's subsidy determination and payment processes. We also reviewed detailed information on the sample of payments covered by the audit for

---

[2]Pub. L. No. 107-300, 116 Stat. 2350 (Nov. 26, 2002).

[3]Pub. L. No. 111-204, 124 Stat. 2224 (July 22, 2010).

[4]GAO, *HUD Rental Assistance: Progress and Challenges in Measuring and Reducing Improper Rent Subsidies*, GAO-05-224 (Washington, D.C.: Feb. 18, 2005) and GAO, *High-Risk Series: An Update*, GAO-07-310 (Washington, D.C.: January 2007).

fiscal year 2010, including the dollar amount and types of errors that internal RHS auditors identified, if any, for each payment. We assessed the reliability of the payment data in the sample by reviewing information on data quality controls and by performing reasonableness checks on the data. We determined that the data were sufficiently reliable for our purposes. In addition, we interviewed RHS officials, including staff responsible for managing the rental assistance program and staff who conduct the improper payments audit, as well representatives from housing industry groups.

To determine the extent to which RHS has complied with applicable requirements and guidance concerning improper payments, we reviewed IPIA and IPERA provisions, associated OMB implementing guidance, and a 2010 presidential memorandum on ensuring payment accuracy. We examined RHS's improper payments audit for fiscal year 2010 and the statistical sampling plan underlying the audit. We also reviewed USDA's Performance and Accountability Reports (PAR) for fiscal years 2008 through 2011 (the most recent available at the time of our review). Our review of RHS's compliance with OMB reporting requirements focused on information in the most recent PAR. Our review of RHS's corrective actions to address payment errors covered information in the PARs for fiscal years 2008 through 2011. Additionally, we interviewed RHS and OMB officials about RHS's efforts to comply with improper payments requirements and guidance.

To determine potential lessons that RHS could learn from HUD's experience, we reviewed HUD's annual studies of improper rental assistance payments (which are comparable to RHS's improper payments audits) conducted for fiscal years 2000 through 2010. We examined HUD's methodology for estimating improper payments and the studies' findings about the sources and magnitude of payment errors. We also reviewed HUD's PARs and other documentation showing the steps the agency had taken to identify, reduce, and recover improper payments and the results of those efforts. Our work emphasized the benefits and challenges associated with HUD's system for verifying tenant incomes because RHS lacks a comparable capability. Finally, we interviewed HUD officials responsible for managing the agency's rental assistance programs and estimating and reducing improper payments. Appendix I contains a more detailed description of our objectives, scope, and methodology.

We conducted this performance audit from July 2011 to May 2012 in accordance with generally accepted government auditing standards.

Those standards require that we plan and perform the audit to obtain sufficient, appropriate evidence to provide a reasonable basis for our findings and conclusions based on our audit objectives. We believe that the evidence obtained provides a reasonable basis for our findings and conclusions based on our audit objectives.

Background

RHS's Rental Assistance Program

The Section 521 rental assistance program, authorized in 1974, is administered by RHS's Multi-Family Housing Portfolio Management Division and its network of state and local offices. The program provides rental assistance for tenants living in properties created through RHS's Multi-Family Direct Rural Rental Housing Loans and Multi-Family Housing Farm Labor Loans programs. These programs provide loans subsidized with interest rates as low as 1 percent to help build rental housing for rural residents and farm workers. Under the rental assistance program, eligible tenants pay up to 30 percent of their income toward the rent, and RHS pays the balance to the property owner.[5] In fiscal year 2011, RHS paid $1.08 billion in subsidies to provide rental assistance to more than 270,000 households residing in 13,211 different properties. RHS pays the subsidies monthly to property owners through multiyear, renewable contracts. The Section 521 program is not an entitlement and, therefore, not all eligible households receive assistance.[6]

Section 521 rental subsidies are based on tenant households' adjusted annual income—that is, gross income less any exclusions and deductions. For purposes of determining adjusted income, the Section 521 program follows the same regulations as HUD's rental assistance programs. These regulations provide for over two dozen types of income exclusions and deductions. For example, income from minors, student

---

[5]Eligible tenants are persons with very low and low incomes, the elderly, and persons with disabilities who are unable to pay the basic monthly rent within 30 percent of their adjusted monthly income. Very low income is defined as below 50 percent of the area median income; low income is from 50 to 80 percent of area median income.

[6]RHS does not collect information on the total number of eligible rural tenants who are not assisted. According to RHS data, about 65,000 tenants living in RHS-subsidized properties pay more than 30 percent of their adjusted monthly income in rent but do not receive rental assistance.

financial aid, and qualifying employment training programs are excluded when determining households' eligibility to receive assistance and calculating rental subsidies. Examples of income deductions include standard deductions for dependents ($480) and elderly and disabled family members ($400) and unreimbursed child care expenses that are necessary for a family member to remain employed.

RHS requires property managers to certify the eligibility of assisted tenants at least annually.[7] As shown in figure 1, property managers do so based on information from tenants on income and applicable exclusions and deductions. RHS policy requires property managers to independently verify this information with third parties. To obtain third-party verification, property managers must directly contact employers, welfare offices, health care providers, and others (depending on what information tenants provide) to ensure that the information is accurate and complete. Property managers must maintain documentation of verified information in the tenant's file and input the information into a Tenant Certification form, which the tenant signs and dates. The property manager then submits the Tenant Certification form to RHS.[8] Property managers must recertify tenants every year, and whenever a tenant's income changes by $100 or more per month, or at the tenant's request whenever the tenant's income changes by at least $50 per month.

---

[7]Property owners may manage the properties themselves or delegate management responsibilities, in full or in part, to a property manager. Unless specifically noted, we use the term property manager to refer to both owners and managers.

[8]Since February 2006, RHS has required all property managers with eight or more units to submit tenant certifications electronically.

Figure 1: Basic Steps in the RHS Rental Subsidy Process, as of April 2012

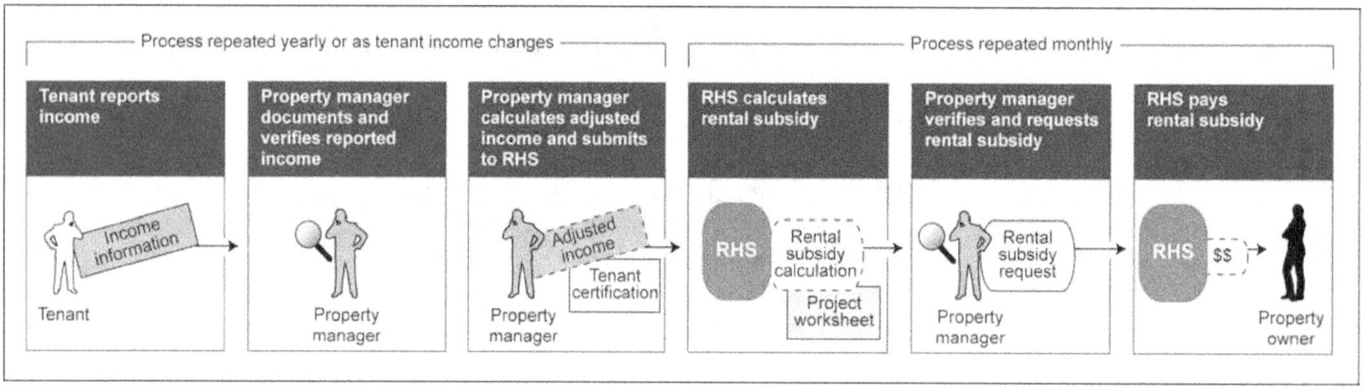

Source: GAO (analysis), Art Explosion (images).

Using information in the Tenant Certification forms, RHS generates Project Worksheets each month. The Project Worksheets document the rent and income levels of tenants for whom the property manager can request rental assistance and calculate the amount of rental assistance due. Property managers review and verify the worksheets via a secure website. As part of this process, the property manager should determine that all rental units are occupied by eligible tenants. According to RHS, information from the Project Worksheets flows into RHS's accounting system, triggering rental subsidy payments to the property owners.

Statutes and Guidance Concerning Improper Payments

RHS's rental assistance program is one of many federal programs subject to requirements set forth in IPIA, as amended. IPIA requires the heads of executive branch agencies to review their programs and activities and identify those that may be susceptible to significant improper payments. The act also requires the Director of OMB to prescribe guidance for agencies to use in implementing IPIA. OMB has issued implementing guidance that requires agencies to use a systematic method for reviewing programs and activities that are susceptible to significant improper payments.[9] IPIA, as amended, and OMB guidance currently define significant improper payments as those that exceed both 2.5 percent of program outlays and $10 million annually, or $100 million regardless of

---

[9]Appendix C (*Requirements for Effective Measurement and Remediation of Improper Payments*) to OMB Circular No. A-123.

the percentage of program outlays. Among other things, the guidance requires agencies to annually estimate improper payments for each susceptible program or activity using statistically valid techniques and to report the results of their efforts to reduce improper payments. Dollar amounts improperly paid can be either positive or negative because errors can reflect overpayments or underpayments. OMB guidance requires using measures of gross error, which reflect the sum of the absolute value of all erroneously paid funds. IPERA amended IPIA in July 2010 by expanding on the previous requirements for identifying, estimating, reporting on, and recovering improper payments. IPERA provisions generally became effective in fiscal year 2011.

HUD's Rental Assistance Programs

Like RHS, HUD provides assistance to low-income renters and is required to estimate and report on improper payments in its rental assistance programs. HUD provides assistance through three major programs: the Housing Choice Voucher and public housing programs, which are administered by HUD's Office of Public and Indian Housing, and project-based Section 8, which is administered by the Office of Housing. The three programs combined had outlays of more than $32 billion in fiscal year 2010. Under each program, HUD makes up the difference between a unit's monthly rental cost (or, for public housing, the operating cost) and the tenant's payment, which is generally equal to 30 percent of the tenant's adjusted monthly income. Public housing agencies (PHA) administer the Housing Choice Voucher and public housing programs, and private property owners administer the project-based Section 8 programs. These program administrators are responsible for ensuring that tenants meet HUD's eligibility criteria and for accurately determining rent subsidies.

In response to growing concerns about improper rental assistance payments, HUD established the Rental Housing Integrity Improvement Project (RHIIP) in fiscal year 2001, with the goal of substantially reducing the estimated dollar amount of improper rent subsidies. To accomplish this goal, HUD initiated three efforts designed to (1) increase monitoring of program administrators (PHAs and property managers), (2) establish an income verification system that allows PHAs and property managers to compare income information reported by tenants with income information from government agencies, and (3) provide additional training and guidance for program administrators.

RHS Has Identified and Reduced Certain Types of Payment Errors, but Its Reported Error Rate May Understate the Magnitude of the Problem

RHS's improper payments audits have identified rental assistance payments that were improper because of incorrectly calculated subsidy amounts and incomplete tenant file documentation. RHS has reported that these types of improper payments have declined since fiscal year 2007; however, RHS's reported estimated error rate may be understated.

RHS Has Identified Improper Payments Caused by Two Types of Errors

Since 2005, RHS has conducted an annual improper payments audit that identifies sources of payment errors and estimates the magnitude of improper payments in RHS's rental assistance program. To complete the annual audit, staff from RHS's Centralized Servicing Center (CSC) examine a random sample of all rental assistance payments made in a given fiscal year.[10] For each rental assistance payment in the sample, CSC staff request the associated tenant file from the property manager and review the file documentation to determine the correct amount of rental assistance that the property owner should have received for that tenant. The CSC staff then compare these calculations with the actual payments in RHS's records to identify any discrepancies and provide RHS's Multi-Family Housing Portfolio Division with a summary of the types and magnitude of errors found in the sample. RHS statisticians project the results of CSC's calculations to the entire universe of rental assistance payments to develop a programwide estimate for improper payments.

In recent years, RHS's improper payments audits have identified rental assistance payments that were improper for two reasons: (1) the property manager incorrectly calculated the amount of tenant income on which the subsidy payment is based and (2) the tenant file did not contain sufficient documentation to support the subsidy payment.

---

[10]CSC services mortgage loans and grants to individuals in rural areas. CSC's Appeals, Audits & Unauthorized Assistance Unit began conducting the improper payments audit starting with the audit of payments made in fiscal year 2007. RHS field staff conducted the audit prior to that time.

- *Incorrect income calculation.* Property managers request rental assistance subsidies from RHS after determining tenants' adjusted monthly incomes. This process involves collecting and verifying income information from tenants and subtracting applicable exclusions and deductions from the tenant's gross income. The rent subsidy is the difference between 30 percent of the tenant's adjusted monthly income and the USDA-approved rent for the unit.[11] As previously noted, RHS regulations provide for numerous types of income exclusions and deductions. Due partly to the number and complexity of these exclusions and deductions, property managers sometimes make errors in calculating adjusted monthly incomes, leading to subsidy payments in the wrong amounts.

- *Insufficient documentation.* The primary documentation required for a payment to be considered proper is the Tenant Certification form, which should be signed and dated prior to the property manager's subsidy request. Among other things, the certification documents a tenant's income, assets, household composition, and disability status. Depending on the tenant's circumstances, other required documents may include documentation of Social Security benefits and medical bills. If a tenant file does not have complete documentation, RHS auditors consider the entire subsidy payment to be improper.

RHS Reported That Its Estimated Error Rate Declined from Fiscal Years 2007 through 2010

RHS reported a decline in its estimated gross error rate (gross improper payments divided by program outlays) from 3.95 percent in fiscal year 2007 to 1.48 percent in fiscal year 2010, the most recent year for which RHS has an estimate.[12] As shown in table 1, this represented a decrease in the estimated dollar amount of gross improper payments from $35 million to $15 million over a period in which total program outlays increased by more than $130 million. The $15 million in estimated improper payments that RHS reported for fiscal year 2010 consisted of $12 million in overpayments and $3 million in underpayments, for a net estimated overpayment of $9 million. Assuming a monthly subsidy payment of $318—the average amount in RHS's sample of fiscal year

---

[11]USDA calculates the rent based on the owners' project costs.

[12]RHS reported that its estimated error rate has a margin of error of 0.97 percent, meaning the actual error rate for fiscal year 2010 could be as low as 0.51 percent and as high as 2.45 percent, with a 99 percent level of confidence.

GAO-12-624 RHS Improper Payments

2010 payments—$9 million is the equivalent of annual subsidy payments to more than 2,300 households.

Table 1: RHS Estimates of Gross Improper Rental Assistance Payments and Error Rates, Fiscal Years 2007-2010

Dollars in millions

Fiscal year audited[a]	RHS rental assistance outlays	Estimated gross improper payments	Estimated gross error rate
2007	$887	$35	3.95%
2008	$887	$18	2.06%
2009	$979	$14	1.39%
2010	$1,020	$15	1.48%

Source: GAO analysis of data in USDA PARs.

[a]The fiscal year audited refers to the year in which the payments examined by the audit were made. The audits are conducted in the year following the year in which the payments were made.

RHS's estimated error rates of 1.39 percent for fiscal year 2009 and 1.48 percent for fiscal year 2010 are below the current IPIA threshold for programs considered susceptible to significant improper payments, but they are close to the revised threshold that will take effect in fiscal year 2013. As previously noted, IPIA, as amended, currently defines significant improper payments as those that exceed both 2.5 percent of program outlays and $10 million annually, or $100 million regardless of the percentage of program outlays. Agencies must estimate improper payments for susceptible programs using a statistically valid methodology and report these estimates to OMB each fiscal year. OMB implementing guidance for IPIA, as amended, will reduce the percentage threshold for susceptible programs from 2.5 percent to 1.5 percent starting in fiscal year 2013. A program with estimated improper payments below the percentage threshold for 2 consecutive years may request relief from the annual reporting requirement. Although RHS's rental assistance program has been below the 2.5 percent threshold for the last 3 years, RHS has not requested relief from OMB on the annual reporting requirement. RHS officials told us they did not plan on requesting relief in the future because annually estimating improper payments and reporting the results has produced useful information that has helped RHS hold property managers accountable for compliance with program requirements.

GAO-12-624 RHS Improper Payments

RHS's Estimates of Improper Payments May Be Understated for Several Reasons

RHS's estimated error rate may be understated because its improper payments audit does not examine some types of errors, excludes improper payments of less than $100 from its error rate estimates, and does not count all payments to tenants with undated certifications as improper.

Unexamined Sources of Errors

RHS's annual audits do not examine three additional sources of payment errors and therefore may understate RHS's error rate (see fig. 2). First, the audits do not check for an improper payment caused by a tenant not reporting all sources of income (intentionally or otherwise). RHS bases its rental subsidies, in part, on income information reported from tenants. RHS policy requires property managers to verify this information with third parties such as employers and welfare offices, but third-party verification may not identify all unreported income (for example, if a tenant discloses income from only one of two part-time jobs). If tenants do not report all of their sources of income, the rental subsidies calculated for the tenants may be too high and result in improper payments.

Figure 2: Potential Sources of Payment Errors Examined and Not Examined by RHS's Improper Payments Audit, as of April 2012

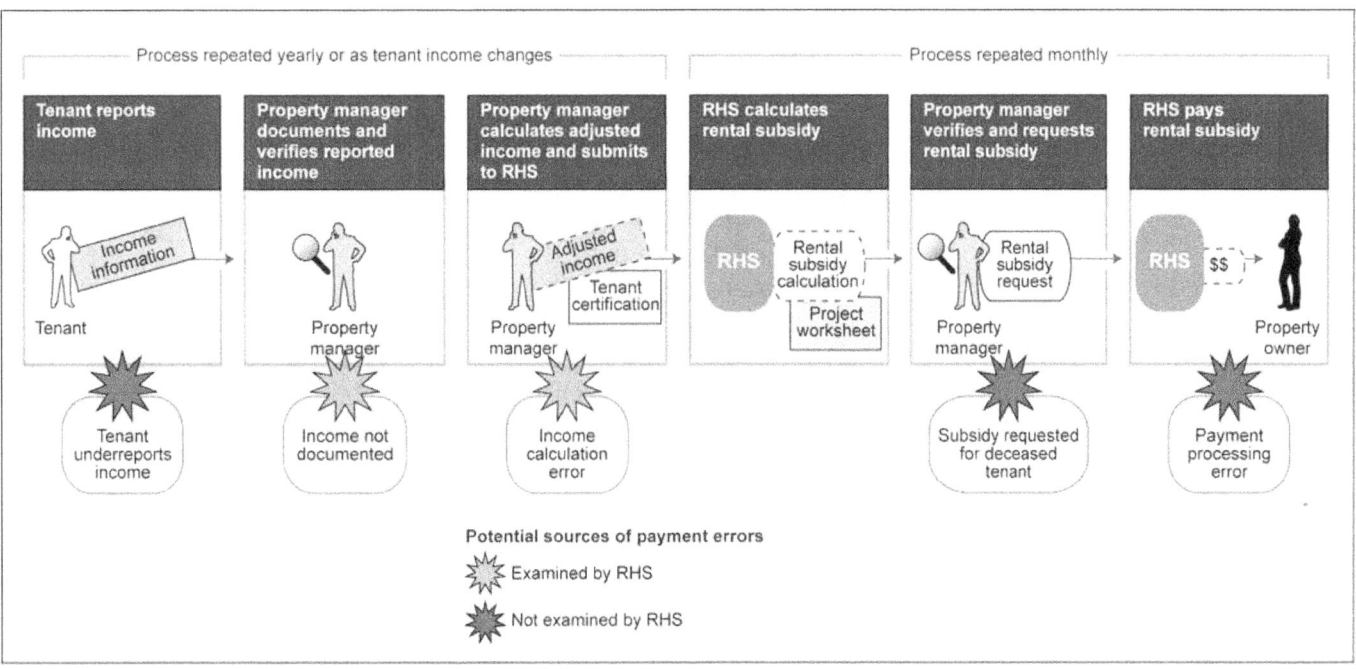

Source: GAO (analysis), Art Explosion (images)

RHS officials told us the improper payments audits do not examine unreported income because RHS does not have access to data that could readily identify unreported amounts. Two sources of such data are the Department of Health and Human Services's (HHS) National Directory of New Hires (New Hires database) and the Social Security Administration's (SSA) data on Social Security and Supplemental Security Income benefits as follows:

- *New Hires database.* This national database compiles information reported by employers to state workforce agencies and information from federal agencies. It contains information on newly hired employees, quarterly wage information for each job held by an employee, and unemployment insurance information on individuals who have received or applied for unemployment. In a prior report, we said that Congress should consider amending the Social Security Act to grant RHS access to the New Hires database for purposes of detecting unreported income.[13] If such access were granted, RHS would have to develop a specific matching agreement with HHS, in accordance with the Computer Matching and Privacy Protection Act of 1988.[14] The President's budget for fiscal year 2013 contains proposed legislation that, if enacted, would give RHS this access. RHS currently has agreements with 31 states that give RHS offices in those states access to state wage data. However, these data have limited value for estimating income reporting errors in the rental assistance program because the data do not provide national coverage. Because the New Hires database is national in scope, it would not present this limitation.

- *SSA benefits data.* RHS officials stated that RHS does not currently have the statutory authority to access data on Social Security and Supplemental Security Income payments to assisted tenants. If granted this access, RHS would have to develop a matching agreement with SSA (pursuant to the Computer Matching and Privacy Protection Act of 1988) in order to use the information. In 2005, USDA's Office of the Inspector General (OIG) recommended that RHS draft legislation that would give RHS access to federal income

---

[13]GAO, *Rural Housing Service: Updated Guidance and Additional Monitoring Needed for Rental Assistance Distribution Process,* GAO-04-937 (Washington, D.C.: Sept. 13, 2004).

[14]Pub. L. No. 100-503.

and benefits databases, including those maintained by SSA.[15] However, RHS officials told us they had been focused on getting statutory access to the New Hires database and had not worked on developing legislation for accessing SSA benefits data. Without this access, future RHS efforts to identify unreported tenant income will be limited.

The second source of improper payments not examined by RHS's audits is a payment made on behalf of a deceased tenant. In the case of single-tenant households, rental assistance should be discontinued when the tenant dies. In the case of multimember households, the amount of rental assistance may need to be adjusted to reflect the change in household composition resulting from a tenant's death.[16] SSA's Death Master File, which is available to federal agencies, is a national database of deceased individuals who had Social Security numbers and whose deaths were reported to SSA. It contains information on date of birth, date of death, and state or country of residence for each decedent, and is a tool for identifying deceased individuals in a timely way. RHS officials told us they had not considered using the Death Master File to help identify improper payments. Therefore, if the deceased tenant's landlord or family does not notify RHS of the tenant's death in a timely manner, RHS could continue to make rental assistance payments on the deceased tenant's behalf.

The third source of improper payments not currently examined by RHS's audits is an error that may occur in payment processing. These errors are discrepancies between the calculated rent subsidy and the amount RHS actually paid. RHS estimated improper payments due to payment processing errors in its audit for fiscal year 2004 but has not done so since then. RHS stopped examining these errors because the fiscal year 2004 audit found them to be insignificant. In addition, RHS officials noted that in 2006, RHS implemented an automated payment processing system to reduce errors in data entry and that 93 percent of subsidies are currently processed through this system. Although the automated system may reduce the likelihood of payment processing errors, 7 percent of payments are not processed through the system. Further, in 2007,

---

[15]USDA, Office of Inspector General, *Rural Housing Service: Subsidy Payment Accuracy in Multi-Family Housing Program*, Report No. 04099-339-AT (March 2005).

[16]A number of factors, including household income and the size of the living unit, determine whether rental assistance payments need to be adjusted following the death of a family member.

USDA's OIG reported on weaknesses in the way RHS was estimating improper payments that may have led RHS to understate its reported error rates in prior years.[17] RHS subsequently changed how it conducts the improper payments audits, such as by using CSC staff (rather than RHS field staff) to help ensure consistency in implementing audit procedures, but it has not reestimated payment processing errors since making these changes. As a result, RHS's assumption that payment processing errors are negligible may not be accurate.

Use of Exclusion Threshold

RHS's estimated error rates may also mask the true extent of improper payments because they exclude improper payments of less than $100. RHS began using the $100 exclusion threshold for its audit of fiscal year 2007 payments. RHS officials said they adopted the threshold for two main reasons. First, RHS officials stated that the $100 exclusion threshold was based on a USDA regulation that lets tenant households wait until their next recertification to report increases in monthly income of less than $100. Second, RHS officials indicated that it was not cost-effective to attempt to recover small improper payments. While the $100 threshold may be appropriate for recertifying tenant income or deciding whether to recover payments, it does not follow that the same threshold is appropriate for conducting the improper payments audit. The purpose of the audit is to measure the magnitude of payments made in error, which IPIA defines as payments that should not have been made or were made in an incorrect amount.

In the fiscal year 2010 sample of 666 payments, RHS found 15 improper payments of $100 or more, which represents 11 percent of all over- and underpayments in the sample. One hundred dollars is substantial in the context of monthly rental assistance payments. To illustrate, an improper payment of $100 represents almost one-third of the median RHS monthly rental assistance payment.

While setting an exclusion threshold that eliminates small amounts from overall error estimates may be reasonable—such as amounts due to rounding up or down to the nearest dollar—RHS's fiscal year 2010 sample shows that using the $100 threshold excludes a high percentage of improper payments from RHS's error estimates, including some larger

---

[17]USDA, Office of Inspector General, *Improper Payments: Monitoring the Progress of Corrective Actions for High-Risk Programs in Rural Housing Service*, Report No. 04601-0014-Ch (March 2007).

errors. As shown in figure 3, 89 percent of the improper payments in the sample were less than $100. Fourteen percent of the improper payments (or 19 payments) were from $25 to $99 and likely cannot be attributed to rounding errors. Additionally, HUD—which is the largest provider of federal rental subsidies—includes all improper payments greater than $5 in estimated error rates for its rental assistance programs. In RHS's payment sample for fiscal year 2010, 51 percent of the improper payments exceeded $5.

Figure 3: Distribution of Improper Payments in RHS's Sample of Fiscal Year 2010 Payments

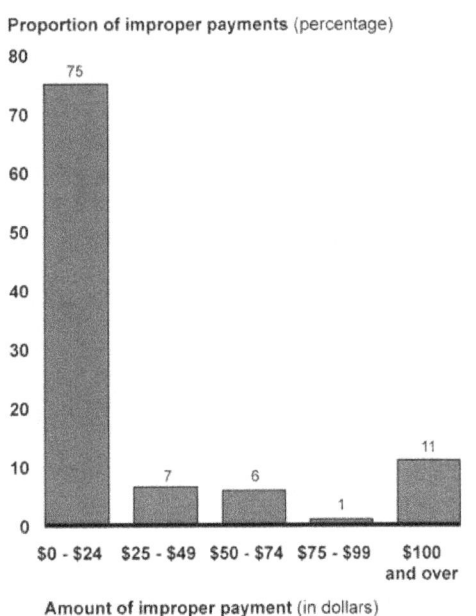

Proportion of improper payments (percentage)

Amount of improper payment (in dollars)

Source: GAO analysis of RHS data.

OMB is required by IPIA to approve the methods used by agencies to estimate improper payments. OMB initially approved RHS's methodology in 2004, prior to RHS's first improper payments audit and 4 years before RHS adopted the $100 exclusion threshold. However, OMB has not subsequently reassessed RHS's methodology and therefore has not examined whether RHS's $100 exclusion threshold is appropriate. In addition, OMB guidance does not address the use of exclusion thresholds. OMB officials told us they generally do not reassess an agency's estimation method unless the agency tells OMB it is making a major change and submits the change to OMB for review. OMB officials also noted that more than 70 programs report on improper payments, which makes regular reassessment of each one challenging. Our analysis of the $100 threshold indicates that RHS's adoption of the threshold did represent a major change. However, RHS did not submit the change to OMB for review.

Our analysis of the payment sample that RHS used for its fiscal year 2010 audit found that the $100 exclusion threshold had a demonstrable impact on the incidence and magnitude of RHS's reported improper payments. If RHS had included all improper payments in its estimates, the estimate of gross dollar errors would have been about $23 million rather than $15 million, and the estimated error rate would have been 2.21 percent rather than 1.48 percent (see fig. 4). RHS's use of an exclusion threshold could affect whether or not the rental assistance program is subject to annual OMB reporting requirements for programs classified as susceptible to improper payments. As previously discussed, OMB has indicated that programs with error rates of at least 1.5 percent in fiscal year 2013 will be classified as susceptible, and our analysis shows that RHS's use of the $100 threshold reduced its error rate below that level for fiscal year 2010.

Figure 4: Estimated RHS Improper Rental Assistance Payments in Fiscal Year 2010 Including and Excluding Errors Less Than $100

Undated Certifications

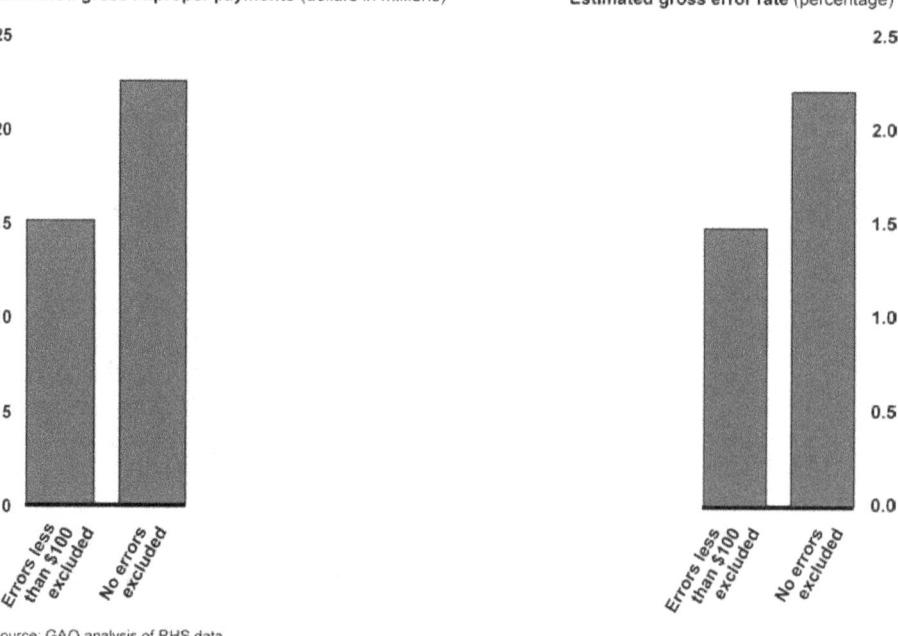

Source: GAO analysis of RHS data.

Finally, RHS's reported error rate may be understated because, contrary to its stated audit procedure, RHS does not always count as improper those payments with Tenant Certification forms that were signed but not dated. The sample of payments that RHS used for the fiscal year 2010 audit contained five payments that were not counted as improper even through the Tenant Certification forms were not dated. Had RHS followed its audit procedure strictly and counted the five payments as improper, the number of improper payments included in RHS's estimate would have increased by one-third, and RHS's estimated error rate would have been 2.53 percent. RHS officials said they did not count payments associated with undated certifications as improper when the auditors were able impute an acceptable certification date from other documents in the tenant file. For example, if auditors determined that income verification documents in the tenant file were current and dated prior to the first subsidy payment request, auditors considered the sampled payment to be proper even though the Tenant Certification form was not dated. While this practice may be reasonable, it is inconsistent with RHS's written audit procedure and reduces the transparency of the audit process. In addition, having unwritten procedures may increase the risk of inconsistent implementation across auditors.

RHS Uses Required Statistical Methods for Estimating Improper Payments but Has Not Fully Met Reporting, Reduction, and Recovery Requirements

RHS has complied with requirements for using statistically valid methods to estimate improper payments and has implemented a number of corrective actions to help address the causes of payment errors. However, RHS's reporting on improper payments has been incomplete, and the agency has not fully utilized techniques cited in statutes and guidance for reducing and recovering improper payments.

RHS Has Complied with Estimating Requirements and Implemented Corrective Actions, but Its Reporting on Improper Payments Has Been Incomplete

RHS's statistical methods for estimating improper rental assistance payments are consistent with OMB requirements. In fiscal year 2011, RHS's reporting on improper payments complied with most OMB requirements but lacked required detail in some areas, including steps for holding agency managers accountable. Additionally, RHS has generally implemented planned corrective actions to address the causes of improper payments.

Estimating Requirements

RHS's methodology for estimating improper payments in its rental assistance program complies with OMB requirements for implementing IPIA, as amended. OMB Circular A-123 requires agencies to base their estimates of improper payments on a random sample of payments that is large enough to yield an estimate with a margin of error of plus or minus 2.5 percentage points at the 90 percent confidence level.[18] Consistent with these requirements, RHS's improper payments audit for fiscal year 2010 reviewed a random sample of 666 payments from a universe of approximately 3.4 million payments. Based on this sample, RHS produced an estimate of gross improper payments with a margin of error of plus or minus 0.97 percent at the 99 percent confidence level, exceeding OMB's standard. Additionally, we found that the techniques and formulas that RHS used to generate the random sample and produce estimates from the payment sample were statistically sound.

Reporting Requirements

To comply with requirements in IPIA, as amended, OMB Circulars A-123 and A-136 state that agencies should include specific information on improper payments in their annual PARs or Agency Financial Reports. As shown in table 2, our review of USDA's fiscal year 2011 PAR found that the information reported for RHS's rental assistance program complied with four of the seven requirements in OMB guidance but only partially complied with the remaining three. For example, the PAR contains required information on the program's estimated improper payments, the causes of improper payments, corrective actions to address these causes, and statutory or regulatory barriers to reducing improper payments. However, the PAR lacks required detail on recovery of improper payments because of delays by USDA in implementing a recovery audit program. In addition, the required discussion of internal

---

[18]Agencies may alternatively use a sample that yields an estimate with a margin of error of plus or minus 3 percentage points at the 95 percent confidence level.

controls, human capital, and information systems to reduce improper payments is limited. The discussion consists of a high-level statement that USDA is creating information systems and infrastructure to reduce improper payments, that some of these efforts are constrained by limited resources, and that USDA is working with OMB to focus resources on critical needs. Because the discussion is not more specific, it is unclear if RHS has sufficiently assessed whether its internal controls, human capital, and information systems are sufficient to reduce improper payments to targeted levels. A USDA representative told us that USDA may provide a more detailed response to this reporting requirement in future PARs. Finally, the PAR does not contain required information on steps and associated timelines for holding RHS managers accountable for reducing and recovering improper payments.

Table 2: RHS Reporting on Improper Payments in Response to OMB Requirements

OMB reporting requirement[a]	Information in USDA's fiscal year 2011 PAR
Requirements met	
The gross estimate of the annual amount of improper payments made in the program and the methodology used to arrive at that estimate.	The PAR provides estimates of the rental assistance program's gross improper payments ($15 million) and error rate (1.48 percent) for fiscal year 2010 (the most recent year for which an estimate has been made). It also describes how RHS selected a random sample of payments for review and how the review was conducted.
A discussion of the causes of improper payments that have been identified.	The PAR cites insufficient file documentation and calculation errors by property owners and management agents as the causes of improper payments in the rental assistance program.
A discussion of corrective actions to address the causes of improper payments, including planned or actual completion dates for these actions.	The PAR indicates that by the end of fiscal year 2011, RHS plans to meet with property managers to provide educational opportunities on the importance of the IPIA process and the types of payment errors identified by RHS. It also states that RHS has ongoing efforts to gain access to HHS's New Hires database (for income verification purposes).
A description of any statutory or regulatory barriers that may limit the agency's corrective actions in reducing improper payments.	The PAR notes that RHS is pursuing access to data, including information maintained by HHS, that RHS could use to verify tenant incomes.
Requirements partially met	
A discussion of the amount of actual improper payments the agency expects to recover and how it will go about recovering them.	The PAR states that USDA is unable to report information on expected recoveries because USDA is in the process of contracting for recovery auditing services. USDA officials told us it would be difficult to estimate recoveries until the recovery audits began.
A discussion of whether the agency has the internal controls, human capital, information systems, and other infrastructure in order to reduce improper payments to the levels the agency has targeted.[b]	The PAR states that USDA is creating information systems and infrastructure to reduce improper payments, but that efforts in some programs are constrained by limited resources. The PAR also notes that USDA is working with OMB to focus available resources on critical needs. However, the PAR does not specifically refer to RHS, its rental assistance program, or internal controls or human capital issues.

OMB reporting requirement[a]	Information in USDA's fiscal year 2011 PAR
A description of the steps the agency has taken and plans to take (including time lines) to ensure that agency managers (including the agency head) are held accountable for reducing and recovering improper payments.	The PAR describes plans developed by RHS state offices that include procedures to train field staff and property managers in maintaining required documentation and verifying tenant incomes. However, the PAR does not describe accountability steps or associated timelines.

Source: GAO analysis of USDA's fiscal year 2011 PAR.

[a]The reporting requirements listed apply to agencies with improper payments estimates that exceed $10 million.

[b]RHS's reduction targets for gross error rates are 1.45 percent for fiscal year 2012, 1.42 percent for fiscal year 2013, and 1.39 percent for fiscal year 2014.

With respect to the accountability issue, OMB guidance requires agencies to describe the steps they have taken and plan to take to hold agency managers accountable for reducing and recovering improper payments. The guidance states that agency managers should be held accountable through annual performance appraisal criteria for meeting applicable improper payments reduction targets and establishing an internal control environment that prevents, detects, and recovers improper payments. However, in response to these requirements, the PAR states only that "[RHS] State Offices with improper payment errors develop a corrective action plan. The plan includes procedures to train field staff, borrowers, and property manager[s] in appropriate required documentation and follow-up with tenants and income-verifiers." While the plans may be key to addressing improper payments, the PAR does not discuss mechanisms for ensuring that agency managers follow through on the plans or how they are held accountable for reducing and recovering improper payments generally. In contrast, the PAR's descriptions of accountability measures for other USDA agencies are more consistent with the OMB guidance. For example, the descriptions for several agencies discuss how improper payments goals and objectives were incorporated into agency managers' performance plans and performance appraisals. RHS officials said that RHS state office directors currently have management goals that emphasize efficient and effective use of resources but acknowledged that improper payments are not specifically referenced in the goals.[19] In April 2012, RHS officials told us they were

---

[19]According to RHS, state office directors have a resource management goal that requires them to (1) develop and execute plans to achieve organizational goals to maximize efficiency and produce high-quality results, and plan, implement, and monitor assigned programs and (2) demonstrate exceptional skills and consistency in making the best use of available resources when faced with changing requirements, critical demands, and the need to do more with less.

seeking departmental approval of revised management goals for fiscal year 2012 that explicitly address improper payments. By not implementing accountability steps for improper payments, RHS may be limiting the effectiveness of its efforts to reduce improper payments. Additionally, by not reporting on accountability steps, RHS is not providing Congress and OMB information they may need for overseeing implementation of IPIA.

RHS Corrective Actions

OMB Circular A-123 requires agencies to develop and implement corrective actions to address the root causes of improper payments. Our review of USDA's PARs for fiscal years 2008 through 2011 and documentation from RHS found that RHS developed and generally followed through on corrective actions over that period (see table 3). RHS's corrective actions included educating property managers about improper payments, enhancing RHS's reviews of improper payments, and seeking access to data for verifying tenant incomes. For example, in 2011, RHS met with housing industry groups about the results of its most recent improper payments audit. This meeting prompted the groups to develop training for property managers on how to reduce improper payments. In 2010, RHS worked with OMB to develop legislation that would grant RHS access to HHS's New Hires database for income verification purposes. The legislative proposal, entitled the "Rural Housing Fraud Prevention Act of 2012," would amend Section 453(j) of the Social Security Act. As previously noted, the proposed legislation was included in the President's budget for fiscal year 2013. Additionally, in 2008, RHS enhanced its triennial supervisory visits (on-site reviews of assisted properties that cover a number of physical, financial, and management issues) to include reviews of tenant files that assess compliance with income calculation and documentation requirements. RHS subsequently enhanced its Multi-Family Information System (MFIS) to track the number and results of these reviews.

Table 3: Status of RHS Corrective Actions Regarding Improper Rental Assistance Payments

RHS corrective actions in USDA's PARs for fiscal years 2008-2011	Status of corrective actions as of March 2012
Inform and provide educational opportunities for property manager business partners about the importance of the IPIA process and the types of payment errors identified by RHS. (2008-2009 and 2011 PARs)	In 2008, RHS sent a letter to the National Affordable Housing Management Association (NAHMA) about the importance of the IPIA process and the results of RHS's improper payments audits. In 2011, RHS met with NAHMA and Council of Affordable Rural Housing representatives about the most recent audit. These groups developed training and educational materials on improper payments and provided training to property managers.
Pursue access to the HHS New Hires database and HUD's Enterprise Income Verification System (EIV) in order to share it with RHS state offices and property managers.[a] (2008-2011 PARs)	RHS sent draft legislation to OMB to obtain access to the HHS New Hires database for purposes of income verification. The President's budget for fiscal year 2013 includes this legislation. RHS officials told us they have met with HUD officials and property managers who use EIV to better understand the system.
Establish a tracking process to monitor the number of tenant files reviewed (e.g., for compliance with income calculation and documentation requirements) during RHS triennial supervisory visits. (2010 PAR)	In 2010, RHS began documenting the number and results of tenant file reviews conducted during triennial supervisory visits and tracking the information in MFIS.
Implement a performance assessment system that reduces management fees paid to property managers who do not comply with RHS requirements (e.g., by making errors in Tenant Certification forms). (2010 PAR)	RHS officials said they put this effort on hold in fiscal year 2012 due to other priorities and the difficulty of integrating information about improper payments into a performance assessment system. RHS officials said they intended to resume this effort in fiscal year 2013.
Implement a quarterly audit process conducted by CSC on selected states' tenant files. (2008 PAR)	Instead of a quarterly audit process, RHS augmented its triennial supervisory visits beginning in 2008 to include reviews of tenant files for compliance with income calculation and documentation requirements.
Follow up on corrective actions for errors identified in the improper payments audit for fiscal year 2008. (2008 PAR)	In 2008, RHS field staff followed up with property managers to confirm they had taken corrective actions to address payment errors identified by the audit.
Issue a letter to the RHS state offices on the findings from the improper payments audit for fiscal year 2008. The letter required state offices with an average error rate of 2 percent or higher during the past 3 years to develop a corrective action plan. (2008 PAR)	In 2008, RHS sent letters to 15 state offices that had average 3-year error rates ranging from 2.4 percent to 7.7 percent. The letters required these offices to develop action plans for reducing payment errors.
Develop a fact sheet for tenants explaining their responsibilities and rights regarding income disclosure and verification. (2008 PAR)	In 2008, RHS issued a fact sheet for property managers to distribute to tenants entitled "Things You Should Know About USDA Rural Rental Housing." The fact sheet emphasizes the importance of submitting and updating accurate income information to property managers and outlines procedures for grieving decisions about benefits.

Sources: GAO analysis of USDA PARs and information from RHS.

[a]EIV is a web-based tool that allows HUD and HUD program administrators to match information on HUD-assisted tenants to the New Hires database and SSA benefits data for purposes of verifying tenant incomes. HUD cannot grant RHS access to EIV because RHS does not have legal access to the New Hires database or SSA benefits data.

RHS Has Not Fully Utilized Techniques for Reducing and Recovering Improper Payments

RHS uses a number of methods to reduce improper payments but has not used a database cited in a 2010 presidential memorandum that could help RHS identify cases in which rental assistance payments should be discontinued or adjusted. In addition, RHS has experienced delays in implementing a recovery audit program to comply with IPERA requirements.

Reducing Improper Payments

OMB Circular A-123 states that federal agencies should take all necessary steps to ensure the accuracy and integrity of federal payments. OMB cites a number of steps that agencies can take to do so, including prepayment reviews, quality-control checks to detect improper payments that may have occurred, and data matching. Also, in June 2010, the President issued a memorandum entitled *Enhancing Payment Accuracy Through a "Do Not Pay List."* The memorandum directs federal agencies to review current prepayment and preaward procedures and ensure that a thorough review of available databases with relevant information on eligibility occurs before the release of any federal funds. The memorandum states that, at a minimum, agencies should check SSA's Death Master File, the General Services Administration's Excluded Parties List System, the Department of the Treasury's (Treasury) Debt Check Database, the HHS OIG's List of Excluded Individuals/Entities, and HUD's Credit Alert System or Credit Alert Interactive Voice Response System.[20] These databases—which constitute the "Do Not Pay List"—can help agencies determine if an individual or entity is ineligible for payments or payments made on their behalf. For example, SSA's Death Master File contains information on deceased individuals who had Social Security numbers and whose deaths were reported to SSA.

RHS has used some of the techniques cited by OMB. For example, as part of their triennial supervisory visits to assisted properties, RHS local offices check the accuracy of rental subsidy calculations and the adequacy of supporting documentation for samples of tenant files. Also, as previously noted, RHS has reached agreements with 31 states that

---

[20]The Death Master File identifies deceased individuals; the Excluded Parties List System identifies suspended or debarred contractors; the Debt Check Database identifies individuals or entities that owe the federal government non-tax debt; the List of Excluded Individuals/Entities identifies individuals and business who have been excluded from participating in federal health care programs; and the Credit Alert System or Credit Alert Interactive Voice Response System identifies individuals who are in default or have had claims paid on direct or guaranteed federal loans, or are delinquent on other debts owed to federal agencies.

give RHS offices in those states the ability to match income information submitted by tenants to state wage data.

However, RHS has not used the "Do Not Pay" databases to check tenant eligibility before making rental assistance payments to property owners.[21] RHS officials told us that they had not considered using the "Do Not Pay" databases for the rental assistance program because some of the databases do not contain information relevant to eligibility for rental assistance and because RHS lacks an automated method for checking rental assistance payments against the databases. Nevertheless, RHS officials acknowledged that some of the information was potentially useful. Additionally, a representative from USDA's Office of the Chief Financial Officer said that USDA agencies currently check some of the "Do Not Pay" databases for some of their programs. The official noted that USDA was in the process of getting access to a Treasury web portal, which was established to meet the requirements of the President's "Do Not Pay" memorandum. The web portal is intended to provide a single point through which federal agencies can access the "Do Not Pay" databases to help determine eligibility for a benefit, grant, or contract award. Treasury offers agencies three options for using the databases: (1) online access, which allows users to compare individual records against the "Do Not Pay" databases via an Internet browser; (2) batch processing, which allows users to send a file to Treasury to compare a large number of records against the databases at one time; and (3) continuous monitoring, which allows users to store files with Treasury and continuously compare the files against the databases.

The USDA representative said his office was in the process of entering into an online processing agreement with Treasury's Bureau of Public Debt, which he indicated will require legal review by USDA's Office of General Counsel. He also indicated that USDA was considering pursuing a batch processing agreement, which would require a separate agreement and legal review. Although RHS officials told us they had not considered the benefits of batch processing for the rental assistance program, a batch processing or continuous monitoring agreement would allow RHS to regularly check tenant records against the Death Master File or other applicable "Do Not Pay" databases. As previously discussed,

---

[21]RHS officials indicated that they use some of the "Do Not Pay" databases to review prospective property owners as part of the approval process for RHS multifamily housing loans.

this matching against the Death Master File could help RHS identify instances in which rental assistance should be terminated or adjusted.

Recovering Improper Payments

USDA has not yet instituted a recovery audit program to implement requirements included in IPERA and OMB implementing guidance. As a result, RHS does not currently have a recovery auditing capability. The process of identifying and recapturing overpayments is known as recovery auditing. IPERA placed increased emphasis on this process by requiring agencies to conduct recovery audits for each program and activity that expends more than $1 million, if conducting such audits is determined to be cost-effective. Previously, requirements for recovery audits were focused on payments to contractors and limited to agencies that entered into contracts with a total value in excess of $500 million in a fiscal year.[22] IPERA decreased the threshold for when recovery audits are required to $1 million in annual outlays and expanded the scope of the audits to include grants, loans, benefits, and other assistance. IPERA allows federal agencies to hire private-sector contract auditors who receive a percentage of the overpayments they collect. OMB guidance states that agencies are to establish and report annual recovery targets, beginning with fiscal year 2011. However, as previously noted, USDA said in its fiscal year 2011 PAR that it was unable to report the amounts it expected to recover because it had not yet awarded a recovery audit contract.

USDA plans to implement a recovery auditing program by hiring a contractor.[23] According to USDA, the agency previously procured recovery audits of contract payments through FedSource (an interagency contracting service that was run by Treasury), but in fiscal year 2010, FedSource closed out the procurement contract USDA had been using.[24] In March 2011, USDA issued a request for proposals (RFP) to solicit the broader range of recovery auditing services required by IPERA. However,

---

[22]IPERA repealed most provisions of the Recovery Auditing Act (Section 831 of Pub. L. No. 107-107).

[23]Although USDA does not have a recovery audit program, it does use authorities under the Debt Collection Improvement Act of 1996 (Pub. L. No. 104-134) to collect monies owed the agency. For example, from 2010 through 2011, RHS reports that it collected more than $1 million in excess rental assistance payments to property owners with RHS multifamily housing loans.

[24]According to USDA, the agency issued task orders against the FedSource contract.

USDA terminated the RFP process after determining the proposals it received did not meet the requirements of its payment recapture/recovery audit plan, which called for an auditing contractor that could cover the breadth of USDA programs and activities. USDA told us that the audit firms that responded to the RFP had experience in contract recovery auditing but lacked sufficient knowledge and experience for IPERA's expanded focus on programs. As a result, USDA did not conduct any recovery audits in fiscal year 2011 and issued a second RFP in August 2011 that specified the department's broader needs. A USDA representative said that the department anticipated awarding a contract in fiscal year 2012 but that it was unclear whether the award would occur in time to report any recoveries in USDA's fiscal year 2012 PAR.

HUD's Efforts Illustrate Potential Benefits and Challenges of Data Matching

HUD's experience in addressing improper payments through data matching may help inform future RHS efforts. HUD has used data matching to estimate and reduce income reporting errors. HUD has also used this technique to terminate and recover assistance to deceased tenants. HUD took several years to develop and implement a data matching system and provides guidance, training, and technical assistance to system users.

Data Matching Has Helped HUD to Identify and Reduce Improper Payments Due to Unreported Tenant Income

HUD uses data matching to help identify and reduce improper rental assistance payments caused by unreported tenant income, also referred to as income reporting error. HUD has used this technique to annually estimate the magnitude of improper payments attributable to income reporting errors. HUD also has developed a web-based data matching tool that gives HUD program administrators (i.e., PHAs and property managers) the ability to determine whether tenants are reporting all sources of earned income. HUD attributes some of the overall decline in its gross improper payments to these efforts.

Estimating Income Reporting Errors

Like RHS, HUD conducts an annual study of improper payments in its rental assistance programs that examines a statistically valid sample of subsidy payments.[25] HUD refers to these studies as quality control studies. HUD's initial quality-control study examined payments in fiscal

---

[25] A HUD contractor carries out the study and documents the results in an annual report entitled *Quality Control for Rental Assistance Subsidy Determinations.*

year 2000, and its most recent study examined payments made in fiscal year 2010. The quality-control studies provide a national estimate of gross improper payments in HUD's three rental assistance programs and estimates for specific sources of payment errors, including income reporting errors, program administrator errors (similar to what RHS would call income calculation and insufficient documentation errors), and billing errors (similar to what RHS would call payment processing errors).[26]

To estimate improper payments due to income reporting errors, HUD developed a methodology that involves data matching. HUD's methodology identifies unreported income sources by comparing information reported by tenants in the quality-control study's sample with information reported by employers in federal databases. The tenant-reported information comes primarily from HUD's tenant databases that capture various household characteristics, including income, documentation from tenant files maintained by program administrators, and interviews with households.[27] The study matches this information with information in HHS's New Hires database and SSA benefits data using tenant Social Security numbers as the key common identifier.[28] As previously discussed, the New Hires database includes nationwide information on both wage and unemployment compensation. The study identifies households that, on the basis of the matching process, appear not to have reported an income source and then takes steps to screen out "false positives." For example, the study eliminates those cases involving unreported income sources, such as income from live-in aides or dependents, which should be excluded from family income under HUD's

---

[26]HUD stated that it does not directly reexamine improper payments due to billing errors each year because the estimated amounts have been small relative to improper payments caused by other types of errors. However, HUD uses baseline estimates of billing errors to derive estimates for other years and includes billing errors in its annual estimates of improper rental assistance payments.

[27]Like RHS, HUD uses standardized electronic forms to collect information on tenants (e.g., income, family composition) for certifying and recertifying program eligibility and stores this information in databases.

[28]SSA benefits include Social Security and Supplement Security Income benefits. For the fiscal year 2000 and 2003 studies, HUD staff performed the matching process using Internal Revenue Service and SSA databases. HUD stopped using the Internal Revenue Service data for matching purposes after it obtained access to the New Hires database. The contractor for the quality-control study currently uses the HUD web-based system discussed later in this section to conduct the matching to the New Hires database and SSA data.

policies. Additionally, the study verifies any unreported income sources by mailing and calling employers and contacting an employment verification service. Finally, the study calculates the correct subsidy amount, based on both the reported and unreported sources of income, and computes the difference between the correct amount and the amount HUD actually paid to estimate the impact of unreported income on HUD's improper payments.

Web-Based Data Matching System

HUD has developed and implemented a web-based tool called the EIV system that allows program administrators to compare income information reported by tenants with income information from government agencies through a secure Internet portal. EIV gives HUD program administrators the ability to independently check the accuracy of reported tenant incomes and identify any income source not disclosed by the tenant during mandatory annual and interim certifications of income.[29]

EIV's data matching capabilities and its use by HUD program administrators have expanded over time. HUD began developing a precursor to EIV in 2004 and initially implemented a system that allowed PHAs to match tenant personal identifiers—Social Security number, last name, and date of birth—against state wage and employment databases, but only in states with which HUD had a matching agreement.[30] To overcome this limitation, HUD received authority that same year under the Social Security Act, as amended, to enter into negotiations with HHS to conduct data matching to the New Hires database (which covers all states) and entered into an interagency agreement with HHS in 2005.[31] In accordance with this authority, HUD initially limited data access to PHAs and negotiated access for property managers after establishing a track record for using and protecting the data. HUD fully implemented the first version of EIV in late 2005, giving PHAs the ability to match to both the New Hires database and SSA benefits data for which HUD had already established a matching protocol in accordance with the process set forth

---

[29]Interim recertifications occur when a tenant experiences a change in income or family composition between annual recertifications. Tenants must be recertified if their monthly income increases by $200 or more a month and can request a recertification if their income declines by any amount.

[30]HUD had agreements with about two dozen states by the end of 2004.

[31]Pub. L. No. 108-199, Jan. 23, 2004.

in the Computer Matching and Privacy Protection Act of 1988.[32] After reaching another agreement with HHS in 2007, HUD expanded access to EIV to property managers. HUD initially made the use of EIV voluntary for program administrators but issued a rule in December 2009 that made use of the system mandatory, effective January 31, 2010.[33]

EIV produces a number of reports that help program administrators to identify unreported income sources and thus help reduce rent subsidy overpayments. For example, the Income Discrepancy Report lists households whose wages, unemployment, or Social Security benefits income reported in EIV is $2,400 or more than the information reported by tenants to HUD. Program administrators must confirm any discrepancies by obtaining information directly from third parties, such as employers, and notify the tenant of the results of the third-party verification.[34] When program administrators determine that a tenant underreported income, they must calculate the difference between the amount of rent the tenant should have paid and the amount the tenant actually paid back to the time the underreporting started. The tenant is obligated to reimburse the program administrator for this difference—potentially through a repayment agreement—and the program administrator is required to send the reimbursed funds to HUD.[35] EIV also produces a New Hires Report that provides employment information on tenants who have started new jobs and, therefore, may have increased their incomes, within the last 6 months. HUD requires tenants to report changes in income when the household's income increases by $200 or more per month. The report allows program administrators to be proactive in reaching out to tenants to report the income changes so that their rents can be adjusted in a timely manner. Timely adjustments reduce the likelihood that the program administrator will make rent subsidy overpayments.

Impact of Using Data Matching to Identify Unreported Income

HUD has indicated that its data matching efforts to identify unreported tenant income have helped to reduce improper payments in the agency's

---

[32]According to HUD officials, before the development of EIV, program administrators accessed SSA benefits data through an existing HUD system.

[33]24 C.F.R. § 5.233.

[34]Program administrators are limited to requesting third-party verification on income the tenant may have received during the past 5 years for which the tenant was assisted.

[35]Tenants who do not agree to repay amounts due are in noncompliance with their lease agreements and may be subject to termination of tenancy or other legal action.

rental assistance programs. HUD estimated that it paid $3.4 billion in gross improper rent subsidies in fiscal year 2000 (out of about $19 billion in outlays), prompting a HUD initiative called RHIIP to address the causes of payment errors. Under RHIIP, HUD established a goal of reducing the dollar amount of payment errors by 50 percent from fiscal years 2000 through 2005. HUD estimated that it had reduced the dollar amount of gross improper payments to $1.5 billion in fiscal year 2005 (out of about $27 billion in outlays), a reduction of over 50 percent. For fiscal year 2010, HUD's most recent estimate, the corresponding amount of gross improper payments was $959 million (out of $33 billion in outlays), which represents a reduction of over 30 percent compared with the fiscal year 2005 estimate.[36]

As previously discussed, HUD also estimates improper payments due to specific sources of payment errors, including income reporting errors. From fiscal years 2004 through 2010, HUD's estimates of improper payments due to income reporting errors ranged from a high of $385 million in fiscal year 2006 (accounting for 1.4 percent of program outlays) to a low of $203 million in fiscal year 2010 (accounting for 0.6 percent of program outlays).[37] However, because of the limited number of unreported income cases in the quality-control study samples, the margins of error around the estimates for income reporting error are too large to know with statistical certainty that income reporting error has declined over time.[38]

---

[36]For its rental assistance programs, HUD reported gross error rates of 17.1 percent for fiscal year 2000, 5.4 percent for fiscal year 2005, and 2.9 percent for fiscal year 2010. These figures are not comparable to RHS's reported error rates because HUD examines sources of errors (e.g., income reporting errors) that RHS does not.

[37]As we previously reported, HUD's fiscal year 2000 estimate of income reporting errors is not comparable to estimates for other years because it used a different methodology. In addition, HUD's subsequent estimate, which covered fiscal year 2003, had a margin of error so large that the estimate was not meaningful. See GAO-05-224.

[38]HUD has indicated that obtaining a more precise estimate of income reporting error would require a considerably large sample but that doing so would be difficult and costly.

Data Matching Has Helped HUD Terminate Assistance for Deceased Tenants and Correct Inaccurate Identifying Information

HUD initially created EIV to verify tenant income and identify unreported income, but it has expanded use of EIV to help monitor other aspects of its rental assistance programs. For example, each month HUD uses EIV to match tenant personal identifiers against SSA's Death Master File. Through this matching process, HUD produces Deceased Tenant Reports, which contain the names of deceased members of tenant households and the dates the deaths occurred, when available. HUD makes these reports available to program administrators through EIV and requires them to access and act upon the reports on a regular basis. Program administrators must first confirm that an individual appearing in the report has died—for example, by contacting the head of household. Program administrators must then terminate assistance on behalf of deceased single-member households, ensure that larger households update information on family composition so the amount of rental assistance can be adjusted, and recover any rental assistance payments made after the tenant died. According to HUD, HUD staff audit program administrators quarterly to confirm that they have stopped making payments on behalf of deceased individuals. Additionally, in fiscal year 2011, HUD indicated that HUD and PHAs recovered $3.5 million in improper payments made to deceased individuals as a result of the Deceased Tenant Reports.[39]

HUD also uses EIV to identify tenants for whom HUD's records do not contain valid or accurate Social Security numbers. According to HUD, correct Social Security numbers are critical to the effective implementation of EIV because the numbers are one of the key personal identifiers used to match tenant information to HHS and SSA data. Through EIV, HUD provides program administrators with Failed Verification Reports that identify tenants whose personal identifying information does not match SSA's records. Program administrators must follow up with tenants in the report to confirm the tenant's Social Security number, date of birth, and last name; obtain documentation from the tenant to verify any discrepant personal identifiers; and correct any discrepant information in HUD's tenant databases. HUD officials told us that these efforts, coupled with 2009 regulations that mandated use of EIV and strengthened HUD's Social Security number disclosure and verification requirements, have substantially reduced the number of

---

[39]According to HUD, the recovered amounts included payments made from fiscal years 2007 through 2011.

tenants who do not match SSA records.[40] According to HUD, this number fell from about 100,000 in January 2009 to less than 30,000 in February 2012.

Developing and Implementing the Data Matching System Has Required Significant Time and Resources

Although HUD has seen benefits from EIV, HUD's experience also shows that developing and implementing such a system poses challenges. These challenges include obtaining data sharing agreements and making information technology investments; implementing regulations, guidance, and training to help ensure effective use of the system; and devoting staff to help ensure effective implementation of the system.

HUD devoted significant time and resources to develop EIV. As previously discussed, after receiving legislative authority to negotiate a data matching agreement with HHS, it took HUD 3 years to reach an agreement that provided data access for all HUD program administrators. HUD had to address a number of issues to alleviate HHS's concerns about data security. For example, HUD had to ensure that (1) only authorized individuals and entities would have access to the HHS data, (2) HUD program administrators were accountable for safeguarding the data, and (3) HUD could track when the data were accessed and by whom. HUD officials estimated that developing EIV, which took place from approximately 2002 through 2007, cost several million dollars. Additionally, HUD estimates that it has spent an average of about $700,000 annually over the last 3 or 4 years for system maintenance and development.

HUD has issued regulations and provided substantial guidance and training about implementing EIV. As previously noted, HUD issued regulations in 2009 that require program administrators to use EIV. The regulations allow HUD to impose penalties against program administrators who do not fully utilize EIV. HUD has also issued, and periodically updates, EIV user, administration, and security manuals. For example, the user manual gives program administrators instructions for navigating EIV and using the data available in the system to make rental subsidy determinations. The security manual sets forth policies and procedures for controlling access to EIV and monitoring system use. In addition, HUD periodically issues notices to program administrators that

---

[40] 24 C.F.R. § 5.216 and § 5.218.

provide detailed guidance on the use of the system and updates on HUD's requirements. HUD disseminates these notices and other EIV user tips via a Listserv®. Further, HUD provides training and technical assistance to program administrators through in-person discussions, webcasts, and presentations at national and regional industry meetings. For example, HUD provides training by webcast at least once or twice a year and has an EIV help desk that can be reached via phone or e-mail.

HUD has staff who are devoted to implementing EIV. HUD's Office of Public and Indian Housing has six headquarters staff dedicated full-time to reviewing EIV reports, monitoring program administrators' utilization of EIV, and identifying and recovering improper rental assistance payments. The Office of Public and Indian Housing also has about 100 EIV coordinators in field offices across the country to provide technical assistance to PHAs, approve requests for access to EIV, and certify the designated EIV users on a semiannual basis. Similarly, HUD's Office of Multifamily Housing (a component of the Office of Housing) has four staff who work part-time on providing EIV technical assistance, program guidance, and training for property managers. In addition, Office of Multifamily Housing staff and entities hired by HUD to administer project-based Section 8 contracts review property owners' and managers' compliance with HUD's EIV requirements as part of annual management and occupancy reviews of assisted properties.

Finally, HUD's experience could potentially inform RHS's future data matching efforts. As previously discussed, development and implementation of EIV involved numerous steps and has required an ongoing commitment of resources. Knowledge of HUD's efforts may help RHS identify the critical tasks it will need to perform if it is able to gain access to federal income data. HUD's experience also highlights the potential benefits to RHS of following through on a data matching program. These benefits include more complete estimates of payment errors and an enhanced ability to reduce and recover improper rental assistance payments.

Conclusions

Congress and the administration have taken a number of steps to help ensure the accuracy and integrity of federal payments. These include enacting IPIA and IPERA, developing guidance for implementing these laws, and issuing a directive on the use of payment eligibility databases. RHS's rental assistance program is one of many federal programs subject to these requirements. RHS's program serves over a quarter of a million low-income tenants and expended more than $1 billion in fiscal year

2011. Because the program is not an entitlement, not all eligible households receive rental subsidies. As a result, subsidy overpayments effectively reduce the resources available to serve the program's target population. Additionally, subsidy calculations can be complex and are based partly on information reported by tenants and collected by property managers. These factors underscore the importance of identifying, reducing, and recovering improper rental assistance payments so that the program can operate as efficiently and effectively as possible.

As required, RHS has made annual estimates of improper payments in its rental assistance program and has implemented corrective actions to help reduce such payments. However, RHS's estimates may be understated for several reasons. In addition, RHS could do more to identify improper payments and strengthen accountability for reducing payment errors as follows:

- RHS is not measuring what may be a significant source of payment errors because it lacks statutory authority to use the New Hires database or SSA benefits data to identify unreported tenant income. Although RHS has drafted legislation that would give the agency access to the New Hires database and has submitted this legislation as part of the President's most recent budget, it has not taken similar steps to obtain access to the SSA data. While HUD's experience points to challenges that RHS may face in using these data—such as negotiating data-sharing agreements and developing appropriate systems, training, and guidance—it also demonstrates benefits. By matching tenant information to these data sources, HUD has been able to identify, and take actions to reduce and recover, substantial amounts of improper payments caused by unreported income and payments to deceased tenants.

- RHS's exclusion of improper payments of less than $100 from its error estimates masks the full extent of payment errors in the rental assistance program. RHS has not provided a strong rationale for its $100 exclusion threshold. Further, the threshold may artificially keep the program's error rate below the 1.5 percent level that will be in effect beginning in fiscal year 2013 and used to identify programs susceptible to significant improper payments. Although adopting the $100 threshold was a major change from RHS's previous method, RHS did not submit the change to OMB, which is responsible for approving agency methodologies for estimation. As a result, RHS lacks assurance that its current approach is appropriate.

- RHS does not have a current estimate of improper payments caused by payment processing errors. As a result, RHS's assumption that these errors are negligible may no longer be valid and may contribute to understatement of the overall error rate estimated for the rental assistance program.

- In RHS's most recent improper payments audit, auditors classified some payments associated with undated Tenant Certification forms as proper, contrary to a written audit procedure. If the auditors had followed the written procedure, instead of the more flexible, unwritten procedure they did use, RHS's estimated error rate would have been higher than reported. While the unwritten procedure may be reasonable, using this procedure reduces the transparency of the audit process and may increase the risk of inconsistent implementation across auditors.

- RHS has not taken advantage of SSA's Death Master File as a tool for identifying improper payments. In contrast, HUD routinely performs matches against the Death Master File to identify and terminate payments made on behalf of deceased tenants and has used this information to recover several million dollars in improper payments. USDA is taking steps to use the Death Master File and other "Do Not Pay" databases through Treasury's web portal, which offers a batch-processing capability. Using this capability for the rental assistance program would enhance RHS's ability to estimate improper payments and allow RHS to regularly check for improper payments made on behalf of deceased tenants.

- RHS has not fully implemented steps to hold agency managers accountable for reducing and recovering improper payments and has not reported on these accountability steps in USDA's PAR. In addition, the PAR does not provide an assessment of whether RHS has the internal controls, human capital, and information systems to reduce improper rental assistance payments to targeted levels. As a result, RHS is not fully complying with OMB guidance and may be limiting the effectiveness of its actions to address payment errors. By correcting these shortcomings, RHS could strengthen accountability in the rental assistance program and better inform Congress and OMB of its efforts to ensure the accuracy and integrity of RHS's payment process.

Matter for Congressional Consideration	Congress should consider amending Section 453(j) of the Social Security Act to grant RHS access to HHS's New Hires database for purposes of verifying tenant incomes. If such access were granted, RHS would need to develop specific procedures with HHS to facilitate it.
Recommendations for Executive Action	To help estimate, reduce, and recover improper payments in the Section 521 rental assistance program, we recommend that the Secretary of Agriculture take the following actions:

- Draft proposed legislation for congressional consideration that would grant RHS access to SSA benefits data for purposes of verifying tenant incomes.

- Submit RHS's methodology for estimating improper payments, including use of the $100 exclusion threshold, to OMB for review.

- Consider examining payment processing errors as part of the next improper payments audit to provide more current information on whether these errors are significant.

- In conducting the annual improper payments audit, either count all payments made on behalf of tenants with signed but undated Tenant Certification forms as improper or revise the audit procedure to classify such payments as proper when an acceptable certification date can be imputed from other documents.

- Complete steps to use SSA's Death Master File—potentially utilizing the batch-processing option offered through Treasury's "Do Not Pay" web portal—to identify improper payments made on behalf of deceased tenants and use this capability in conducting the annual improper payments audit and for ongoing oversight of program payments.

- Complete steps to ensure that RHS managers are held accountable for reducing and recovering improper payments in the rental assistance program and include a discussion of the accountability steps in USDA's PAR.

- Include a discussion in USDA's PAR of whether RHS has the internal controls, human capital, information systems, and other infrastructure to reduce improper rental assistance payments to targeted levels.

Agency Comments and Our Evaluation

We provided a draft of this report to the Acting Director of OMB and the Secretaries of Agriculture and Housing and Urban Development for their review and comment. We received oral comments from OMB on May 18, 2012. We received written comments from USDA's Under Secretary for Rural Development. We also received technical comments from USDA, which we incorporated where appropriate. HUD did not provide comments on the draft report.

In their oral comments, OMB staff said a recommendation in our draft report that was directed to OMB would be better directed to USDA. Our draft report contained a recommendation that OMB review RHS's methodology for estimating improper payments, including use of the $100 exclusion threshold. Although OMB staff agreed that a reassessment of RHS's methodology was appropriate, they said their process was to undertake such a reassessment only after an agency submitted its methodology to OMB for review. Therefore, we modified our recommendation to state that USDA submit RHS's estimation methodology to OMB for review. We provided the modified recommendation to USDA in time for USDA to consider it in preparing written comments on our draft report.

In its written comments, USDA said it generally agreed with the recommendations in our report, but it did not comment on specific recommendations. USDA cited various actions RHS had taken, which we described in our draft report, to reduce improper rental assistance payments and secure access to HHS's New Hires database. USDA also reiterated that RHS had no plans to abandon improper payments audits or seek an audit exemption from OMB even if the rental assistance program's error rate falls below OMB's reporting threshold. Additionally, USDA stated that it "appreciated GAO's notation that the RHS IPIA error rate is lower than that of the U.S. Department of Housing and Urban Development, even including RHS's errors under $100." Although our draft report did contain RHS's estimated error rate for fiscal year 2010 (including and excluding errors less than $100) and a footnote in a separate section showing HUD's estimated error rate for the same year, our report did not compare the error rates of the two agencies. Such comparisons are inappropriate because RHS's error rate does not include sources of errors that HUD's does include, such as income reporting errors and billing errors. In our final report, we added language to the footnote containing HUD's error rate to emphasize this point.

GAO-12-624 RHS Improper Payments

As agreed with your offices, unless you publicly announce the contents of this report earlier, we plan no further distribution until 30 days from the report date. At that time, we will send copies to the appropriate congressional committees, the Secretary of Agriculture, the Secretary of Housing and Urban Development, the Acting Director of the Office of Management and Budget, and other interested parties. In addition, the report will be available at no charge on the GAO website at http://www.gao.gov.

If you or your staff members have any questions about this report, please contact me at (202) 512-8678 or sciremj@gao.gov. Contact points for our Offices of Congressional Relations and Public Affairs may be found on the last page of this report. GAO staff who made key contributions to this report are listed in appendix III.

Mathew J. Scirè
Director, Financial Markets
    and Community Investment

Appendix I: Objectives, Scope, and Methodology

Our objectives were to examine (1) the extent to which the Rural Housing Service (RHS) has examined the sources and magnitude of improper rental assistance payments; (2) the extent to which RHS has complied with applicable requirements and guidance for estimating, reporting, reducing, and recovering improper payments; and (3) potential lessons RHS could learn from the Department of Housing and Development's (HUD) efforts that have helped to identify and reduce improper rental assistance payments.

Sources and Magnitude of Improper Payments

To determine the extent to which RHS has examined the sources of error for improper rental assistance payments, we reviewed RHS's annual improper payments audits for fiscal years 2004 through 2010 (the most recent audit available at the time of our review) and the U.S. Department of Agriculture's (USDA) Performance and Accountability Reports (PAR) for fiscal years 2007 through 2011, which summarize information from the improper payments audits. We reviewed RHS's policies and procedures for determining and processing rental subsidy payments to identify steps in the subsidy process where improper payments can occur. We also reviewed provisions in the Improper Payments Information Act of 2002 (IPIA), as amended, and Appendix C of Office of Management and Budget (OMB) Circular A-123 to determine the types of payments that should be classified as improper. To supplement our understanding of the sources of improper rental assistance payments, we interviewed RHS officials and representatives from the Council for Affordable Rural Housing and the National Affordable Housing Management Association.

To determine the extent to which RHS has examined the magnitude of improper rental assistance payments, we reviewed the improper payments audits and PARs cited previously. We used this information to analyze trends in RHS's estimated gross improper payments and gross error rates from fiscal years 2007 through 2010. We focused on that time frame because RHS used a somewhat different methodology and had different types of personnel conducting the audits prior to that period. For example, the audit for fiscal year 2007 marked the point at which staff from RHS's Centralized Servicing Center (CSC), rather than RHS field staff, began performing the audits. We also reviewed Appendix C of OMB Circular A-123 to determine OMB's thresholds for identifying programs that are susceptible to significant improper payments. We compared RHS's error estimates with the current OMB thresholds and the thresholds that will take effect in fiscal year 2013.

We performed a more detailed analysis of the payment errors found in the
improper payments audit for fiscal year 2010 by obtaining and reviewing
an RHS database containing the 666 randomly selected payments
reviewed by CSC auditors. Among other things, the database included
the dollar amount and types of errors, if any, that the auditors identified
for each payment. We reviewed CSC's written audit procedures and
examined the extent to which CSC followed them, including criteria for
classifying payments as improper. We also interviewed CSC officials
about how they conducted the audit and their reasons for any deviations
from written audit procedures. Additionally, we interviewed RHS officials
about how they used the results of the audit to make programwide error
estimates and their rationale for excluding payments of less that $100
from these estimates. Using information in the database, we determined
the proportions of improper payments that fell within different ranges,
including above and below RHS's $100 exclusion threshold and above
and below HUD's $5 exclusion threshold. We calculated what the
estimated amount of gross improper payments and the gross error rate
would have been for the rental assistance program if RHS had included
all improper payments in its estimates and compared these figures with
the ones RHS reported.[1] We interviewed OMB officials about RHS's
exclusion threshold and the extent to which they had reviewed or
provided guidance to RHS on its estimation methodology, including the
threshold. We also reviewed IPIA provisions describing OMB's
responsibilities for reviewing agency estimation methodologies.

To assess the reliability of the data in the database of 666 sampled
payments, we conducted reasonableness checks, including tests for
missing data and outliers, on key data elements that RHS used to
estimate improper payments. In addition, we reviewed RHS
documentation about the database and interviewed RHS staff responsible
for maintaining the data. Because RHS drew the payment sample from
RHS's Multi-Family Information System, we also reviewed the processes
RHS had in place to safeguard the accuracy and reliability of data in the
system. On the basis of this review, we determined that the data in the

---

[1]More specifically, to produce a programwide estimate without the $100 threshold, we
calculated the absolute value of all improper payments in the payment sample and
multiplied this amount by the number of times the sample size was represented in the total
population of rental assistance payments. We divided the result by RHS's total rental
assistance outlays for fiscal year 2010 to estimate the gross error rate.

database of sampled payments were sufficiently reliable for purposes of
our analysis.

Compliance with Requirements Concerning Improper Payments

To determine the extent to which RHS complied with applicable
requirements and guidance concerning improper payments, we reviewed
provisions in IPIA, as amended; associated OMB guidance; and various
RHS and USDA documents. To determine whether RHS met
requirements for estimating improper payments, we reviewed Appendix C
of OMB Circular A-123, which contains specific rules for sampling
payments and the level of precision that error estimates must have. We
compared these requirements with information presented in RHS's
improper payments audit for fiscal year 2010, the statistical sampling plan
underlying the audit, and USDA's fiscal year 2011 PAR. In addition, we
reviewed the techniques and formulas RHS used to generate its fiscal
year 2010 payment sample and produce estimates from the sample and
found them to be statistically sound. To assess whether RHS met
reporting requirements, we examined Appendix C of OMB Circular A-123,
as well as OMB Circular A-136, which set forth specific information that
agencies should include in their annual PARs about improper payments.
We reviewed USDA's fiscal year 2011 PAR to determine the extent to
which it contained the required information. Because the reporting
requirements call for agencies to identify corrective actions they have
taken or plan to take, we also identified RHS corrective actions described
in USDA's PARs from fiscal years 2008 through 2011 and determined the
status of those actions as of March 2012. We reviewed information
regarding these corrective actions, including RHS correspondence, draft
legislation, and other documents, as well as reporting by USDA's Office of
the Inspector General (OIG). We also interviewed RHS and OMB officials
about RHS's efforts to comply with improper payments requirements and
guidance.

To assess RHS's use of required or recommended techniques to reduce
and recover improper payments, we reviewed guidance contained in
OMB Circular A-123, a 2010 presidential memorandum on ensuring
payment accuracy through a "Do Not Pay List," and provisions in IPIA, as
amended by the Improper Payments Elimination and Recovery Act of
2010 (IPERA). We reviewed documentation—including USDA PARs,
RHS improper payments audits, and USDA OIG reporting—describing
the methods RHS has used to help reduce improper payments. We also
interviewed RHS officials and a representative from USDA's Office of the
Chief Financial Officer about these methods, including the use of
databases that constitute the "Do Not Pay List." With regard to RHS's

recovery of improper payments, we reviewed USDA's PAR for fiscal year 2011, which contains a summary of USDA's efforts to implement the recovery audit provisions in IPERA. We also reviewed USDA's payment capture/recovery audit plan and fiscal year 2011 requests for proposals to solicit the services of a recovery auditing contractor. Finally, we interviewed RHS officials and a representative from USDA's Office of the Chief Financial Officer about the status of establishing a recovery audit program in response to IPERA.

Potential Lessons Learned from HUD

To determine the potential lessons RHS could learn from HUD's efforts to reduce improper payments, we reviewed HUD's quality-control studies of improper rental assistance payments (which are comparable to RHS's improper payments audits) conducted for fiscal years 2000 through 2010. We also reviewed information in HUD's PARs for fiscal years 2001 through 2011, which summarize the results of these studies and describe HUD's corrective actions to address the causes of improper payments. We used information from the PARs to examine trends in HUD's estimated gross improper payments and gross error rate from fiscal years 2000 through 2010. Additionally, we reviewed findings from our prior work on HUD's efforts to reduce payment errors and interviewed officials from HUD's Offices of Public and Indian Housing, Multifamily Housing, and Policy Development and Research about their more recent efforts.

Our work emphasized the benefits and challenges associated with HUD's web-based Enterprise Income Verification System (EIV) because RHS lacks a comparable capability for verifying tenant incomes through data matching. To determine the specific benefits of EIV, we reviewed supplements to HUD's quality-control studies that focus specifically on the data matching component of the studies and provide estimates of improper payments due to income reporting errors. We analyzed changes in HUD's estimates of income reporting errors from fiscal years 2000 through 2011. However, we could not draw statistically valid conclusions about the changes, because the small number of households in HUD's samples with unreported income resulted in estimates with large margins of error. We also reviewed information on HUD's use of EIV to identify and recover payments to deceased tenants and to correct inaccurate tenant identifying information. Additionally, we interviewed the HUD officials cited previously about the benefits they had seen from using the system to annually estimate improper payments and help ensure the integrity of rental assistance payments on an ongoing basis. To determine the challenges associated with developing and implementing EIV, we reviewed information from HUD about how EIV evolved, the agency's efforts to negotiate data matching agreements with the Department of Health and Human Services, estimated costs for developing and maintaining the system, and staff resources dedicated to implementing EIV and monitoring its use by program administrators. Further, we reviewed HUD regulations, guidance, manuals, and training materials that HUD developed to help implement EIV. Finally, we interviewed HUD officials about these various efforts.

We conducted this performance audit from July 2011 to May 2012 in accordance with generally accepted government auditing standards. Those standards require that we plan and perform the audit to obtain sufficient, appropriate evidence to provide a reasonable basis for our findings and conclusions based on our audit objectives. We believe that the evidence obtained provides a reasonable basis for our findings and conclusions based on our audit objectives.

United States Department of Agriculture
Rural Development
Office of the Under Secretary

MAY 2 1 2012

Mr. Matthew J. Scirè, Director
Financial Markets and Community Investment
U.S. Government Accountability Office
441 G Street, NW
Washington DC 20548

Dear Mr. Scirè:

Thank you for providing the U.S. Department of Agriculture (USDA) Rural Development (RD) and Rural Housing Service (RHS) with the Government Accountability Office (GAO) draft report entitled "Efforts to Identify and Reduce Improper Rental Assistance Payments Could Be Enhanced," Report Number GAO-12-624. We appreciate the opportunity to respond to GAO's review of RHS's compliance with the Improper Payments Information Act (IPIA) requirements for the Rental Assistance Program. The agency generally agrees with the recommendations in this report. For your consideration, USDA offers the following comments and requests that a copy of these comments be included in the final report.

We are very pleased GAO found that the "RHS methodology for estimating improper payments in its rental assistance program complies with OMB requirements for implementing IPIA, as amended." RHS worked very hard to improve accountability in the Rental Assistance Program. USDA will submit a legislative proposal to Congress entitled "Rural Housing Fraud Prevention Act of 2012." This legislation will authorize USDA's access to earnings information currently available through the U.S. Department of Health and Human Services' (HHS) National Directory of New Hires, which contains wage data reported by employers. This information will be used to verify earnings data provided by tenants renting rural multi-family housing program units, as well as, applicants, borrowers, and grantees of rural housing loans or grants administered by USDA-RD. Our efforts to secure access to the HHS New Hires database are evidence of our commitment to reducing waste, fraud and abuse in our subsidy program, and we appreciate the support GAO noted for RHS access to this information.

Additional steps taken by RHS to further reduce the incidents of improper payments include: changing the auditing procedure in 2008 to strengthen audit integrity; enhancing the Triennial Supervisory Visit procedure to identify random subsidy payments made in error; conducting on-going discussions with industry groups to encourage improper payment training; and providing transparency in the RHS-issued, and publicly-available, IPIA reports that detail audit findings. We believe these steps demonstrate our commitment to closely monitor program performance and continued program auditing, despite the technological matching limitations identified in the report. RHS has no plans to abandon the audit procedure or seek an audit exemption from the Office of Management and Budget (OMB), even if the program error rate falls below OMB's reporting threshold requirement.

1400 Independence Ave., S.W. • Washington, DC 20250-0700
Web: http://www.rurdev.usda.gov

Committed to the future of rural communities.
"USDA is an equal opportunity provider, employer and lender."
To file a complaint of discrimination write USDA, Director, Office of Civil Rights,
1400 Independence Avenue, S.W., Washington, DC 20250-9410 or call (800) 795-3272 (Voice) or (202) 720-6382 (TDD).

RHS's commitment to error rate reduction extends beyond the National Office headquarters and reaches out to the Multi-family Housing Program field staff. USDA's field structure allows for closer monitoring and review of property manager and owner compliance as field staff is better able to pinpoint property management weaknesses, such as site manager turnover, that require increased training and closer review for subsidy calculation mistakes. In addition, we appreciate GAO's notation that the RHS IPIA error rate is lower than that of the U.S. Department of Housing and Urban Development, even including RHS's errors under $100. We believe this speaks directly to the hard work of our field staff.

RHS, and the rest of USDA, will consider GAO's recommendations to modify the procedural methodology for program administration and improper payment auditing. As noted in the report, USDA's Office of the Chief Financial Officer is quickly moving toward utilization of various "Do-Not-Pay" databases, and continues to work toward successful award of a contract for a Departmental recovery auditing program.

Once again, we appreciate the opportunity to respond to GAO's report on RHS's compliance with the IPIA requirements, and we hope that our comments will help in the preparation of the final report. If you have any questions, please contact Mr. John Purcell, Director, RD Financial Management Division, at (202) 692-0328.

Sincerely,

Dallas Tonsager
Under Secretary
Rural Development

Appendix III: GAO Contact and Staff Acknowledgments

GAO Contact	Mathew J. Scirè, (202) 512-8678 or sciremj@gao.gov
Staff Acknowledgments	In addition to the individual named above, Steve Westley (Assistant Director), Jeremy Conley, Isidro Gomez, John Lord, John McGrail, Marc Molino, Dae Park, Jennifer Schwartz, Verginie Tarpinian, and Heneng Yu made key contributions to this report.

GAO's Mission	The Government Accountability Office, the audit, evaluation, and investigative arm of Congress, exists to support Congress in meeting its constitutional responsibilities and to help improve the performance and accountability of the federal government for the American people. GAO examines the use of public funds; evaluates federal programs and policies; and provides analyses, recommendations, and other assistance to help Congress make informed oversight, policy, and funding decisions. GAO's commitment to good government is reflected in its core values of accountability, integrity, and reliability.
Obtaining Copies of GAO Reports and Testimony	The fastest and easiest way to obtain copies of GAO documents at no cost is through GAO's website (www.gao.gov). Each weekday afternoon, GAO posts on its website newly released reports, testimony, and correspondence. To have GAO e-mail you a list of newly posted products, go to www.gao.gov and select "E-mail Updates."
Order by Phone	The price of each GAO publication reflects GAO's actual cost of production and distribution and depends on the number of pages in the publication and whether the publication is printed in color or black and white. Pricing and ordering information is posted on GAO's website, http://www.gao.gov/ordering.htm. Place orders by calling (202) 512-6000, toll free (866) 801-7077, or TDD (202) 512-2537. Orders may be paid for using American Express, Discover Card, MasterCard, Visa, check, or money order. Call for additional information.
Connect with GAO	Connect with GAO on Facebook, Flickr, Twitter, and YouTube. Subscribe to our RSS Feeds or E-mail Updates. Listen to our Podcasts. Visit GAO on the web at www.gao.gov.
To Report Fraud, Waste, and Abuse in Federal Programs	Contact: Website: www.gao.gov/fraudnet/fraudnet.htm E-mail: fraudnet@gao.gov Automated answering system: (800) 424-5454 or (202) 512-7470
Congressional Relations	Katherine Siggerud, Managing Director, siggerudk@gao.gov, (202) 512-4400, U.S. Government Accountability Office, 441 G Street NW, Room 7125, Washington, DC 20548
Public Affairs	Chuck Young, Managing Director, youngc1@gao.gov, (202) 512-4800 U.S. Government Accountability Office, 441 G Street NW, Room 7149 Washington, DC 20548

Please Print on Recycled Paper.